vocal /piano

michael bublé crazy love

ISBN 978-1-4234-9099-9

HAL•LEONARD®
CORPORATION
7777 W. BLUEMOUND RD. P.O. BOX 13819 MILWAUKEE, WI 53213

Visit Hal Leonard Online at
www.halleonard.com

CRY ME A RIVER

Words and Music by
ARTHUR HAMILTON

* Recorded a half step higher.

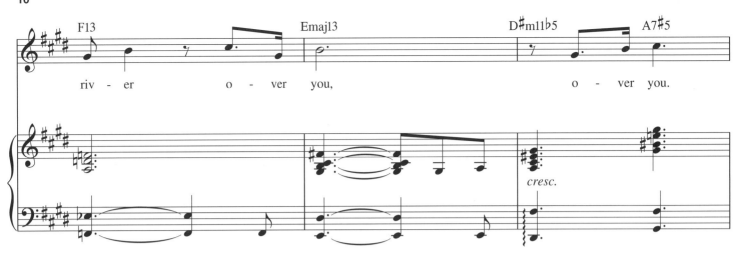

riv - er o - ver you,   o - ver you.

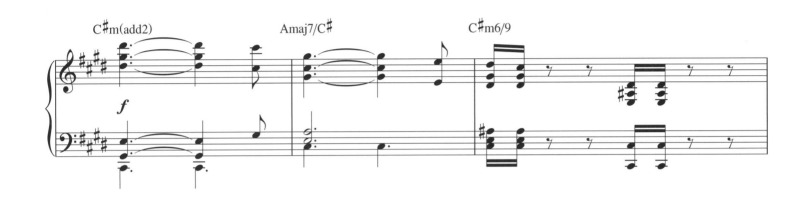

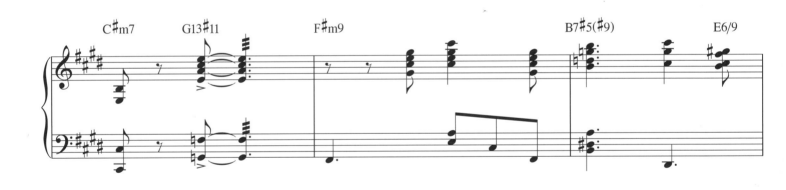

You say you love me, but you lied. _____

ALL OF ME

Words and Music by SEYMOUR SIMONS
and GERALD MARKS

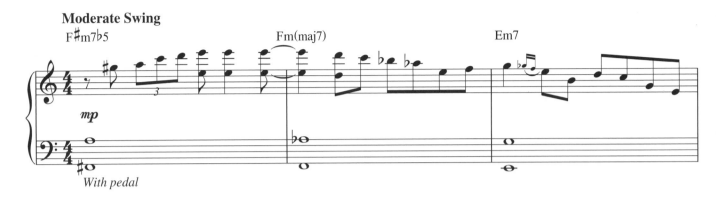

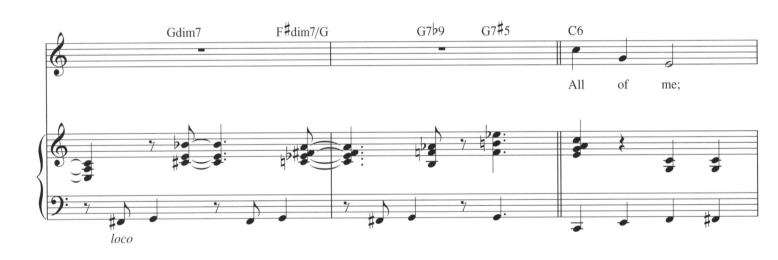

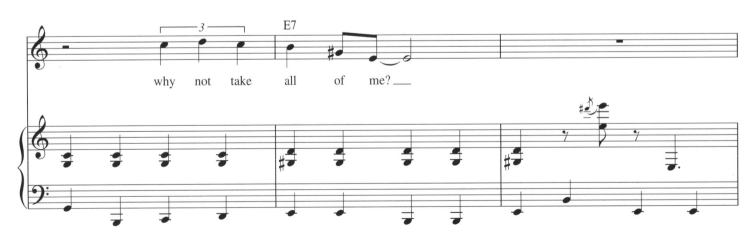

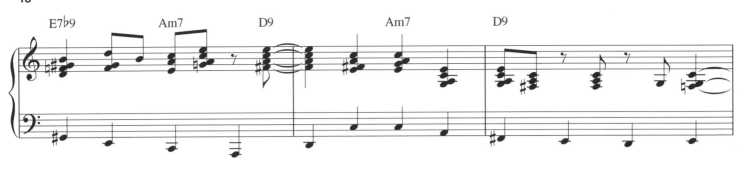

Your good-bye

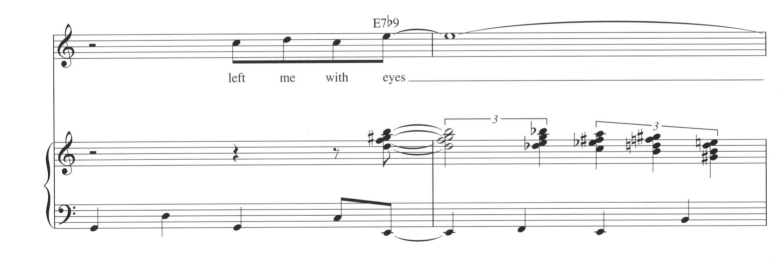

left me with eyes

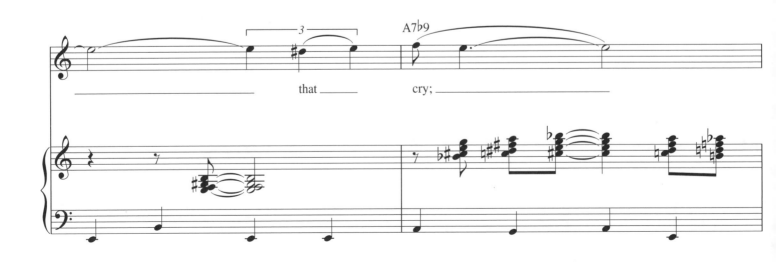

that _____ cry;

All of me; _____ why not take all of me? _____

_____ Can't _____ you see I'm _____ a mess

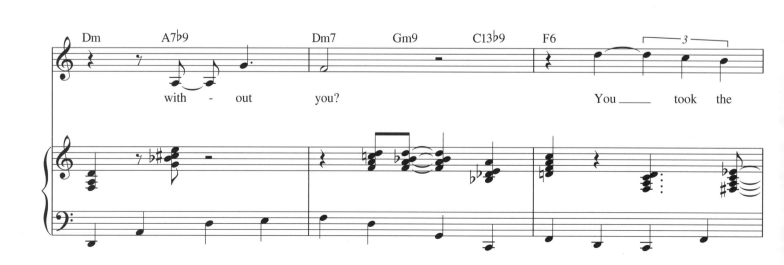

with - out you? You _____ took the

GEORGIA ON MY MIND

Words by STUART GORRELL
Music by HOAGY CARMICHAEL

CRAZY LOVE

Words and Music by
VAN MORRISON

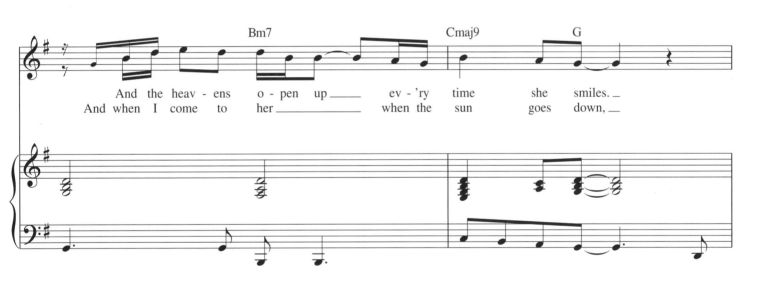

love, love, love, love, cra - zy love. *Instrumental solo*

Solo ends Yes, I need her in ___ the day - time, ___

(Doo doo doo doo doo ___ doo doo.) ___

HAVEN'T MET YOU YET

Words and Music by MICHAEL BUBLÉ,
ALAN CHANG and AMY FOSTER

* Recorded a half step higher.

get it right___ and we'll be u – nit – ed._____

And I know that we can

ALL I DO IS DREAM OF YOU

Words by ARTHUR FREED
Music by NACIO HERB BROWN

Recorded a half step higher.

HOLD ON

Words and Music by MICHAEL BUBLÉ,
ALAN CHANG and AMY FOSTER

52

HEARTACHE TONIGHT

Words and Music by JOHN DAVID SOUTHER,
DON HENLEY, GLENN FREY and BOB SEGER

Moderate Shuffle

Some-bod-y's gon-na hurt some-one__ be-fore the night is through.__
some-bod-y

Some-bod-y's gon-na come un - done;___

Well, we can beat a - round the bush - es, we can

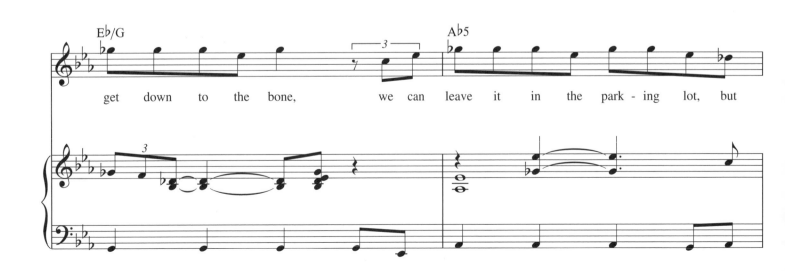

get down to the bone, we can leave it in the park - ing lot, but

YOU'RE NOBODY 'TIL SOMEBODY LOVES YOU

Words and Music by RUSS MORGAN,
LARRY STOCK and JAMES CAVANAUGH

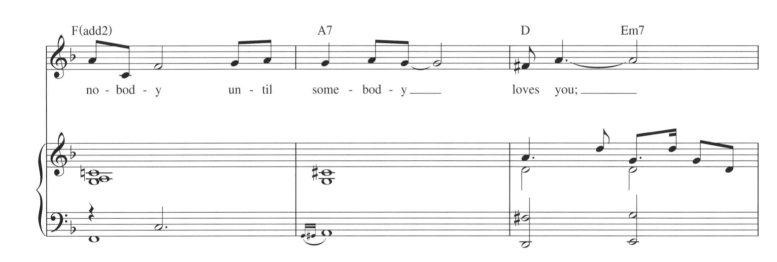

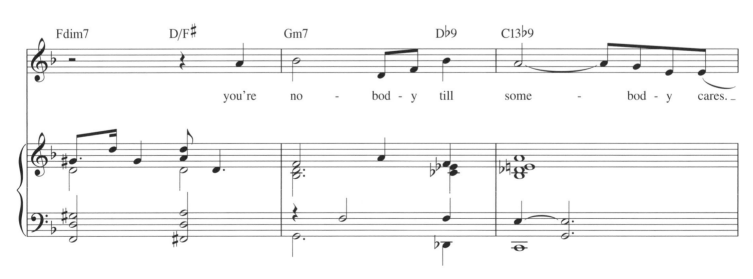

BABY
(You've Got What It Takes)

Words and Music by CLYDE OTIS
and MURRAY STEIN

Moderate Motown Shuffle

two hearts a cook - in' to make a ___ fi - re grow. ___
some - bod - y spe - cial to knock me ___ off my feet. ___

And, ___ ba - by, you've got what it takes. ___

You know, it

I ___ said,

ooh. _____

AT THIS MOMENT

Words and Music by
BILLY VERA

STARDUST

Words by MITCHELL PARISH
Music by HOAGY CARMICHAEL

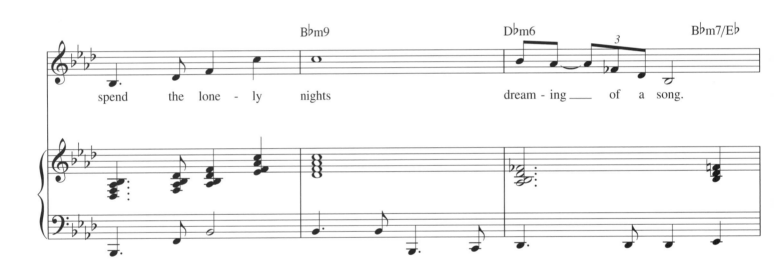

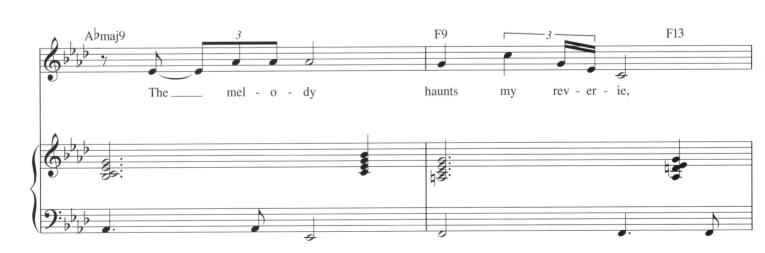

WHATEVER IT TAKES

Words and Music by
RON SEXSMITH

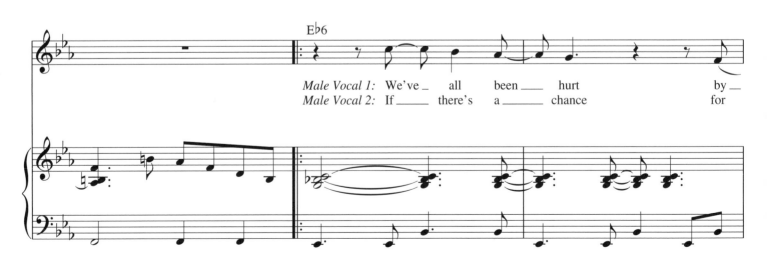

Male Vocal 1: We've all been hurt by

Male Vocal 2: If there's a chance for

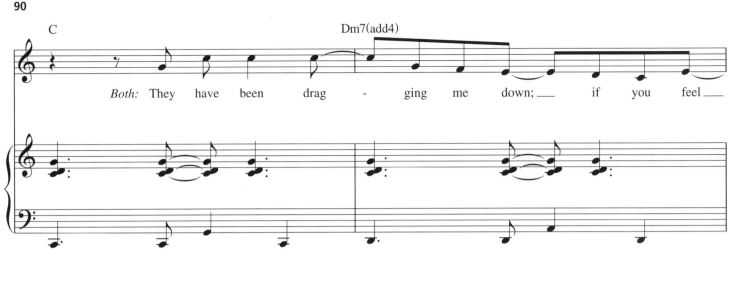

Both: They have been drag - ging me down; ___ if you feel ___

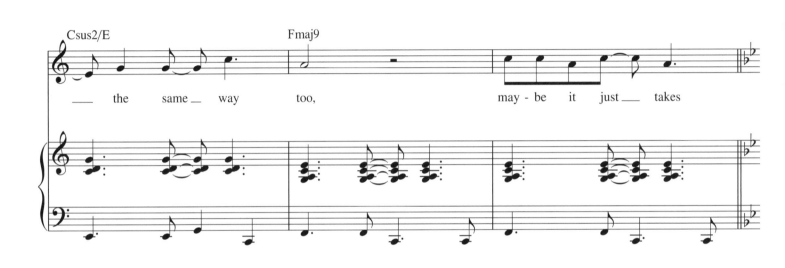

___ the same ___ way ___ too, may - be it just ___ takes

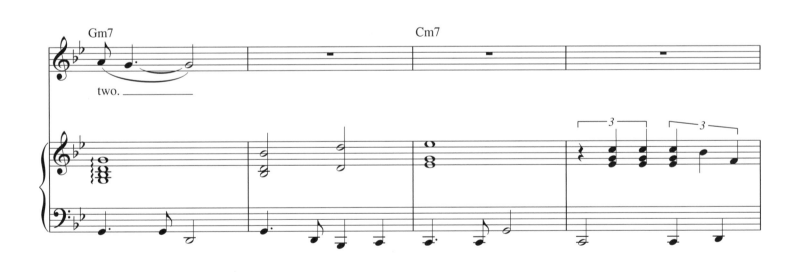

two. ___

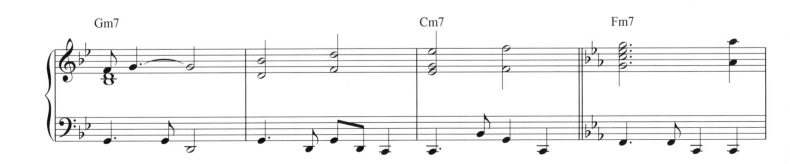